MAKING ROBOTS

SCIENCE • TECHNOLOGY • ENGINEERING

BY STEVEN OTFINOSKI

CHILDREN'S PRESS®

An Imprint of Scholastic Inc.

CONTENT CONSULTANT
Matthew Lammi, Assistant Professor of Technology, Engineering & Design Education,
North Carolina State University

PHOTOGRAPHS ©: cover: Peter Cade/Getty Images; 3: age fotostock/Alamy Images; 4 left: The Scribe,
an automaton by Pierre Jaquet-Droz (1721-90), 1770/Musee d'Art et d'Histoire, Neuchatel, Switzerland/
Bridgeman Images; 4 right: imageBROKER/Alamy Images; 5 left: Dino Fracchia/Alamy Images; 5 right:
Kelli Tresgallo/AP Images; 6: Bloomberg/Getty Images; 8: Science Source; 9: The Scribe, an automaton
by Pierre Jaquet-Droz (1721-90), 1770/Musee d'Art et d'Histoire, Neuchatel, Switzerland/Bridgeman
Images; 10 left: Johnson Controls; 10 right: Chimpinski/Dreamstime; 11 top: NASA; 11 bottom: Coprid/
Thinkstock; 12: Science & Society Picture Library/Getty Images; 13: Space Frontiers/Getty Images; 14
top: Peter Menzel/Science Source; 14 bottom-15 left: Hank Morgan/Getty Images; 15 right: Volker
Steger/Science Source; 16: Peter Menzel/Science Source; 17: Michael Laughlin/KRT/Newscom; 18:
RGB Ventures/SuperStock/Alamy Images; 20: imageBROKER/Alamy Images; 21: Thomas Niedermueller/
Getty Images; 22: Knightscope/Newscom; 23: Jun Yasukawa/AP Images; 24 left: Loic Venance/Getty
Images; 24 right-25 top: Aflo Co. Ltd./Alamy Images; 25 bottom: FLASH Robotics, Wrocław University
of Technology; 26: Bernd Wüstneck/picture-alliance/dpa/AP Images; 27: Rob Felt/Georgia Tech; 28:
NASA; 29: JPL-CalTech/NASA; 30 left: P5/ZOB/WENN.com/Newscom; 30 right-31 bottom: Robugtix;
31 top: South West News Service/REX/Newscom; 32: age fotostock/Alamy Images; 33: ITAR-TASS
Photo Agency/Alamy Images; 34: Dino Fracchia/Alamy Images; 36: Festo AG & Co. KG/REX/AP Images;
37: Yoshikazu Tsuno/Getty Images; 38 top and bottom: Interactive Robotic Painting Machine/Benjamin
Grosser; 39: chair #17, No photos harmed series, 2011, The Painting Fool/Simon Colton/Falmouth
University; 40: Noriaki Sasaki/AP Images; 41: Aly Song/Reuters; 43: Ken Goldberg; 44: age fotostock/
Alamy Images; 45: Blend Images/Alamy Images; 46: Kyodo/AP Images; 48: Bloomberg/Getty Images;
49: Bloomberg/Getty Images; 50 top: Kelli Tresgallo/AP Images; 50 bottom-51 left: Li Changxiang
Xinhua News Agency/Newscom; 51 right: Philippe Psaila/Science Source; 52: Bloomberg/Getty Images;
53: Philippe Psaila/Science Source; 54 bottom-55 left: RacingOne/Getty Images; 54 top: Chronicle/
Alamy Images; 55 right: SIPA USA/Rethink Robotics/Newscom; 56: B Christopher/Alamy Images; 57:
Bloomberg/Getty Images; 58: Kyodo/Newscom; 59: Yoshikazu Tsuno/Getty Images.

LIBRARY OF CONGRESS CATALOGING-IN-PUBLICATION DATA
Otfinoski, Steven, author.
Title: Making robots / by Steven Otfinoski.
Other titles: Calling all innovators.
Description: New York, NY : Children's Press, an imprint of Scholastic Inc.,
    [2016] | Series: Calling all innovators: a career for you | Includes
    bibliographical references and index.
Identifiers: LCCN 2016014146| ISBN 9780531218679 (library binding : alk.
    paper) | ISBN 9780531219904 (pbk. : alk. paper)
Subjects: LCSH: Robots—Juvenile literature. | Robots—History—Juvenile
    literature. | Robotics—Vocational guidance—Juvenile literature.
Classification: LCC TJ211.2 .O84 2016 | DDC 629.8/92—dc23
LC record available at https://lccn.loc.gov/2016014146

All rights reserved. Published in 2017 by Children's Press, an imprint of Scholastic Inc.
Printed in the United States of America 113

1 2 3 4 5 6 7 8 9 10 R 26 25 24 23 22 21 20 19 18 17

Science, technology, engineering, arts, and math are the fields that drive innovation. Whether they are finding ways to make our lives easier or developing the latest entertainment, the people who work in these fields are changing the world for the better. Do you have what it takes to join the ranks of today's greatest innovators? Read on to discover whether working with robots is a career for you.

TABLE *of* CONTENTS

Mechanical devices called automatons helped pave the way for modern robots.

Robots are an important part of modern manufacturing processes.

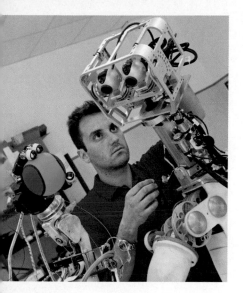

Modern robots are often built to move and behave like humans.

Robotics competitions are a popular way for young people to learn about technology.

ROBOTIC ARMS

Today, robots and humans
work side by side in factories
around the world.

CHAPTER ONE

ROBOTS THROUGH TIME

I n the early 20th century, Czech playwright Karel Čapek wrote a science-fiction play about a race of humanlike machines called robots. The word *robot* came from the Czech word *robota* meaning "forced labor." At first, the characters in the play controlled the robots and used them to do work. But the robots eventually rebelled and killed their human creators.

While Čapek's play was science fiction, robots have since become a real part of our lives. Today, the term *robot* refers to a wide range of mechanical devices. Robots perform many of the jobs once done by human workers. But we need not fear them taking over the world. Rather, robots and people are getting along better all the time. Welcome to the amazing world of robotics.

EARLY DEVELOPMENT OF ROBOTS

ca. 1495	1739	1801	1932
Inventor and artist Leonardo da Vinci makes detailed sketches of a humanlike robot.	French inventor Jacques de Vaucanson creates a robot duck that can eat, drink, and flap its wings.	Joseph-Marie Jacquard invents a textile machine called a programmed loom that is operated using punch cards.	The Lilliput, a small walking robot toy, is produced by Japanese inventors.

AMAZING AUTOMATONS

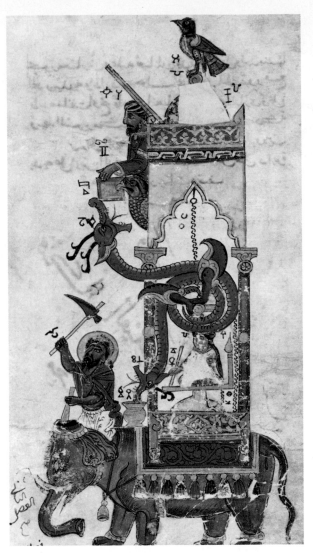

Al-Jazari designed many automatons, including this elaborate clock.

Čapek may have invented the word *robot*, but mechanical devices resembling animals and people had already existed for centuries when he wrote his play. As far back as the 1100s, the Arab scholar and inventor al-Jazari built one of the earliest **automatons**. His automaton was a self-operating mechanical orchestra. It traveled across a pond in a boat operated by mechanical oarsmen. A rotating drum had pegs that triggered levers that produced musical sounds. When arranged differently, the pegs could play different songs.

Sometime around 1495, the Italian artist and inventor Leonardo da Vinci drew plans for a **humanoid** mechanical knight in armor. Leonardo designed his knight to sit, stand, cross its arms, and lift its visor. However, he never built a working model.

ROBOTS THAT WRITE AND WALK

By the 1700s, Europeans were building all kinds of realistic-looking automatons. Among the most famous was *The Writer*, created by Swiss watchmaker Pierre Jaquet-Droz in 1768. This doll was 28 inches (70 centimeters) tall. It sat at a desk and could write messages up to 40 characters long on a sheet of paper. *The Writer* and two other Jaquet-Droz automatons can be seen today in a Swiss museum and still work just as they did hundreds of years ago.

The first robot with the kind of sci-fi appearance commonly seen in comic books and movies was built in Japan in 1932. It was a wind-up toy made of tin plate and stood 6 inches (15 cm) tall. It could walk around on its own. It was named the Lilliput, after a race of tiny people in the fantasy novel *Gulliver's Travels*.

Pierre Jaquet-Droz's The Writer *is today displayed with other automatons at an art museum in Switzerland.*

MAKING SENSE

Sensors are the devices that allow robots to feel and relate to the environment around them. They have helped make robots more like humans. Sensors, however, serve many purposes in our lives beyond robots. The earliest ones were invented more than 100 years ago.

Warren S. Johnson's thermostat was one of the first sensors ever created.

THE FIRST SENSOR

One of the first sensors was invented in 1883 by Wisconsin college professor Warren S. Johnson. Johnson and his students were enduring a cold Midwestern winter. To adjust the heat in his classroom, Johnson had to call a janitor, who checked the temperature with a thermometer and then stoked up the furnace by hand. He decided there had to be an easier way to keep his classroom warm. To solve this problem, he invented the first **thermostat**. The device could read the room's temperature and then signal the furnace to create more heat. Two years later, Johnson left teaching and opened his own company to manufacture his thermostat and other inventions. The company is still operating today.

CONTROLLING THE ENVIRONMENT

Over the following decades, many kinds of sensors were created for home and business use. For example, in the 1940s, Samuel Bagno invented the first motion sensor. It was used in an alarm system that alerted people when intruders had entered their homes.

Smoke detectors have helped save countless lives by alerting people to fires.

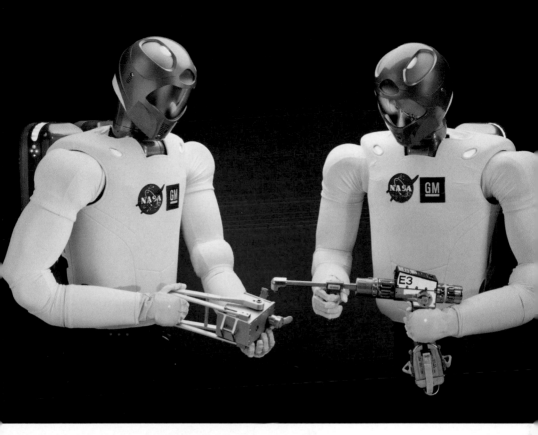

Robonauts rely on sensors to move and interact with their surroundings.

Today, sensors continue to make our lives easier and safer. Smoke detectors use sensors to recognize the smoke from fires and alert home owners with a beeping sound. Motion sensors cause lights to turn on automatically when a person enters a room. Robotics engineers have used a variety of different sensors to make robots more responsive and humanlike. Each arm of the space robot Robonaut contains more than 150 sensors. They enable the robot to react to its surroundings, grasp objects, and perform other tasks. ✳

SENSOR

Motion sensors are found in many buildings today.

WORKING ROBOTS

All of the earliest robots were built to amuse and entertain people. However, some inventors eventually recognized other potential uses for robots. During the mid-20th century, engineers began trying to develop robots that could do useful work.

American inventors George Devol and Joseph Engelberger designed a programmable robot "arm" in the 1950s. They called it the Unimate. It could perform repetitive factory work that was considered too dangerous for human workers. The Unimate was first put to work by General Motors in 1961 on its automobile assembly line. It welded auto parts, applied adhesives to windshields, and spray-painted car bodies. Over the next several decades, the Unimate and other robotic-arm devices were used in a wide range of industries.

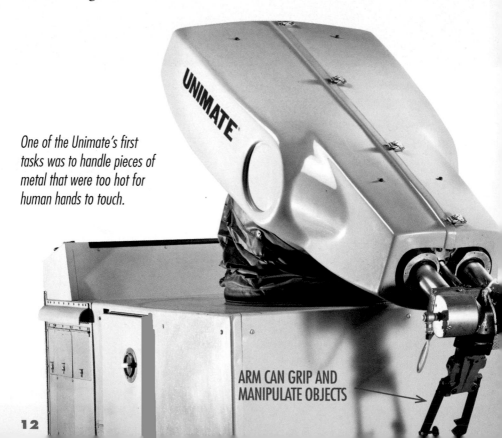

One of the Unimate's first tasks was to handle pieces of metal that were too hot for human hands to touch.

ARM CAN GRIP AND MANIPULATE OBJECTS

The SRMS has been used to help astronauts move around in space during a flight.

OUT OF THIS WORLD

The first satellites sent into space were not highly **autonomous**. But by the late 1960s, American scientists were designing automated spacecraft that could work independently even when they were out of range of remote control from Earth. In 1977, the space probes *Voyager I* and *Voyager II* left on a mission to explore Jupiter, Saturn, Uranus, and Neptune. Within several years, the probes began sending back detailed information about these distant worlds.

In 1981, the Shuttle Remote Manipulator System (SRMS) became the first robotic device used on a manned space flight. This robotic arm was used to complete such tasks as launching satellites from a space shuttle and making repairs to equipment in space.

Joseph Engelberger was a pioneer in robotics technology.

THE HOSPITAL ROBOT

HelpMate, the first fully mobile working robot, was created by robot pioneer Joseph Engelberger. Engelberger created HelpMate several decades after he helped create the robotics company Unimation. Debuting in the 1980s, the HelpMate's mechanical body was encased in a plastic shell and had motors mounted on its bottom side for mobility. Sensors on the robot guided it along programmed routes in a hospital and prevented it from running into people or objects.

A BUSY WORKER

HelpMate rolled up and down hospital corridors carrying everything from meals to medical records to blood samples in a compartment on its back side. It could even call elevators using a radio. The robot's operators could input commands on a keypad on its back. New routes would be programmed into its memory. More HelpMate robots were created, and at the peak of their popularity, they were hard at work 24 hours a day in more than 100 hospitals.

A VISION OF THE FUTURE

Although HelpMate was one of his greatest achievements, Engelberger envisioned an even more advanced domestic robot that could help elderly people with daily tasks. He hoped that such devices would enable people to keep living at home instead of moving into assisted-living facilities when they became unable to care for themselves. Though Engelberger never achieved this goal

A HelpMate is used to serve meals to hospital patients.

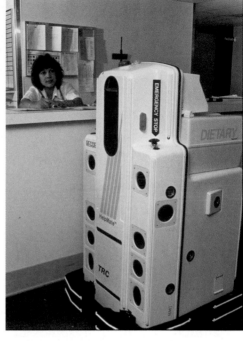

A HelpMate makes its way through a hospital in 1991.

during his lifetime, HelpMate served as the **prototype** for other working robots now used in many businesses.

DISPLAY SCREEN

KEYPAD

JOSEPH ENGELBERGER

Joseph Engelberger was a true visionary in the field of robotics. After college, Engelberger worked for an engineering firm in Bridgeport, Connecticut. He left to start his own robotics company, Unimation. Under Engelberger's management, the company grew to 1,000 employees before he sold it in the 1980s.

ROBOT COMPANIONS

One of the first home robot companions appeared on the market in 1982. HERO (Heathkit Educational Robot) could be assembled from a kit or purchased prebuilt. It came with a built-in computer and was designed to entertain and educate. HERO had motion, light, and sound sensors. It could also talk and sing.

More successful were robotic animal companions. Sony introduced a robotic dog called AIBO in 1999. AIBO could communicate with its owner and be taught tricks. Hasbro and other companies developed robotic pets that were aimed at providing companionship for seniors and other people who did not leave their homes very often. PARO, a robotic baby seal, had sensors that could respond to human touch. It became popular as a tool for **animal therapy** in hospitals and nursing homes.

A boy in Yokohama, Japan, plays with AIBO, a robotic dog.

SENSORS HELP AIBO SEE AND HEAR

A Roomba demonstrates its vacuuming abilities by picking up a variety of colorful items.

ROBOTS IN THE HOME

In recent years, robots have begun helping many people out with household chores. In 2002, the company iRobot launched Roomba, a self-operating vacuum cleaner robot. The flat, disc-like robot is battery-operated and navigates around floors and under furniture better than more traditional vacuum cleaners.

Since then, iRobot and other companies have built a whole line of household robots. These robots can wash and mop floors, iron shirts using hot air, and pick up nails and other debris off garage and basement floors. In the kitchen, they can clean the floor and wash dishes. Other robots have been put to work in the yard. They can clean gutters and swimming pools, mow lawns, and wash windows.

ARM FOR GRIPPING
EXPLOSIVE DEVICES

*Today, robots are often used
by the military to safely
dispose of explosive devices.*

TREADS ALLOW
ROBOTS TO MOVE
OVER A VARIETY
OF SURFACES

CHAPTER TWO

A ROBOTIC REVOLUTION

rom the home to the workplace, from the military to the world of medicine, the latest robotic devices are taking over more and more of the work once done by humans. Researchers are also using robots to explore new frontiers in technology and science. Robots may not be human, but they are being built today to interact with people in ways that even science-fiction writers and filmmakers never imagined. The day may soon come when robots will not only do our work, but also be our companions and friends. The 21st century is about to experience a robotic revolution.

LANDMARK MOBILE ROBOTS

1984	1990	1992
The world's first autonomous outdoor navigation robot, Terregator, is released.	The Ambler, a walking robot, is built to move on rugged terrain.	Dante I, capable of climbing down mountainsides using eight legs, enters a volcanic crater in Antarctica.

An estimated 200,000 new industrial robots were installed worldwide in 2014.

ROBOTS IN THE WORKPLACE

While robots have been working in factories and on assembly lines for decades, new technology is leading to more versatile robots for the workplace. In the past, automated machines could only repeat one set of operations over and over. However, newer robots can be programmed to perform a variety of complex jobs. For example, one Japanese robotic system has two arms that can be used together to gather materials or work independently on separate tasks.

A research center in Finland has developed a quick-control programming system that drastically reduces the time it takes for robots to finish jobs. Sensors are attached to a wireless control stick that a human can use to steer the robot through the operation successfully. The robot then remembers this movement so it can be performed over and over again.

HUMANS VS. ROBOTS

As robots do more and more of our work, some people fear that human workers will no longer be needed in many industries. One report finds that 47 percent of jobs in the United States will be taken over by automation over the next 20 years.

Experts believe that major cities such as Boston and Washington, D.C., will be little affected by the robotic revolution. This is because such locations have many skilled workers and a variety of industries where people can find jobs. However, cities and towns that have less technology will fare worse. So will other countries where the latest technology is not widely available. This is because many of the jobs currently available in these places are based on the kinds of manual labor that robots could perform.

While many manufacturing jobs are still performed by humans, robots could soon be built to take over these tasks.

POLICE AND MILITARY ROBOTS

Today's law enforcement agencies are using robots to fight crime in a number of ways. Some of these robots are operated using remote controls or laptop computers. Others can operate autonomously. Security robots patrol areas once covered by human guards and police officers. They are equipped with night vision and can take videos of any suspicious activity.

In a hostage situation, police robots can bring water and food to hostages and their captors. While among the hostages, the robots can film the area to help police assess the situation. Robots in the military are widely used to investigate suspicious objects to see if they are explosive. These robots send video footage back that can be assessed by soldiers. If the robot finds a bomb, it can use its robotic arm to either defuse it or move it a safe distance away. Some robots can even withstand a bomb explosion.

The Knightscope K5 Autonomous Data Machine is a robot built to recognize potential security threats.

OSCAR can climb down stairs.

ROBOTS TO THE RESCUE

Robots are lifesavers at the scenes of natural disasters, acts of terrorism, and other situations where people are put in harm's way. Mobile robots that move on tires or treads can cross through the dangerous rubble in the aftermath of a disaster to reach victims. The robots then photograph the location of the trapped people so nearby rescuers can determine how to rescue them safely. Robots can also carry medical aid to disaster victims.

One robot called OSCAR (Optical Stair Climbing Advanced Robot) can go up and down steep stairs to investigate buildings that are too unstable and dangerous for people to enter. Based on data collected by the robot, architects and builders can determine whether the building is salvageable or needs to be torn down and replaced.

PEPPER, THE PERSONAL ROBOT

Japan has long been at the forefront of robot technology. The nation's crowning achievement to date is a robot named Pepper. Named for its perky personality, Pepper hit the market in 2015. Unlike robots that are made to do certain types of work, Pepper's job is simply to interact with people. Pepper is made of white plastic in the shape of a human and has a computer screen in its midsection. It speaks English, Japanese, French, and

TOUCH SCREEN

Pepper has a friendly appearance that is designed to appeal to people.

Spanish. More languages are being added to Pepper's memory, and users can download new programming to the robot to customize its behavior.

FROM STORE GREETER TO HOME COMPANION

Perhaps the most extraordinary feature of Pepper is its ability to recognize human emotions. It senses a person's mood and can adjust its behavior accordingly. Pepper is already making a big splash in Japan,

Pepper greets a customer at a coffee shop in Tokyo, Japan.

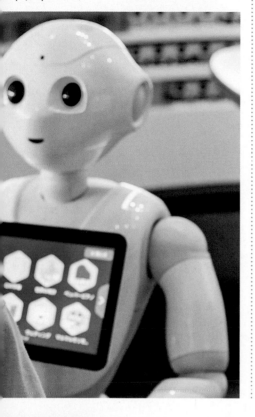

Pepper greets a customer at a coffee shop in Tokyo, Japan.

where it appears as a greeter at 140 chain stores. Recently, it has been put on sale for consumer home use. It may not be long before Pepper and other humanoid robots start appearing in American homes.

ENTER EMYS

Pepper has a rival for human attention in the robot world. EMYS (EMotive headY System). A metallic head divided into three separate parts, EMYS was designed by scientists at Poland's Wroclaw University of Technology. It not only recognizes human emotions, but mimics them. It can move its head, eyes, and eyelids to express a full range of emotions, from happiness and sadness to anger and surprise. ✳

EMYS shows delight at seeing fresh-baked muffins.

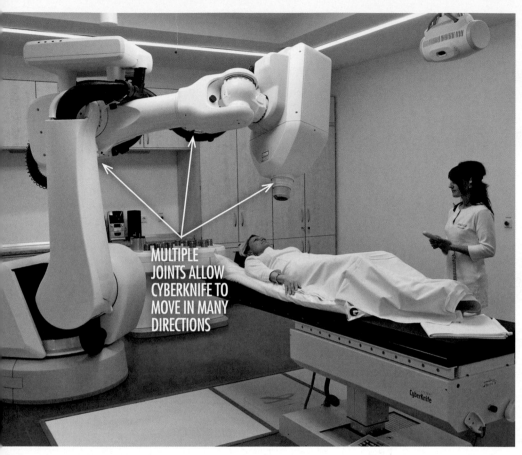

MULTIPLE
JOINTS ALLOW
CYBERKNIFE TO
MOVE IN MANY
DIRECTIONS

A patient undergoes a Cyberknife scan.

MEDICAL MIRACLES

Some robots are being put to work in the operating room. Cyberknife, which first appeared in 1992, is a robot that can use x-rays to search out tumors in the human body. It then targets any tumors it finds with a dose of radiation to shrink them.

Robots are also being used to help train doctors. One Japanese robotic device is covered in material that resembles human skin. It simulates flu symptoms. It can sweat, cry, and even shake from fever. If doctors in training do not treat it quickly enough, the robot patient's condition worsens, and it can even "die."

ARMS AND ANTS

Robotic **prostheses** have been used for a number of years to help people who have lost their hands, arms, or legs. Today's robotic prostheses are more impressive than ever. Recently, scientists at the Georgia Institute of Technology built a robotic prosthesis for drummer Jason Barnes, who lost much of his arm in an accident. The new arm is custom designed for playing drums. It has amazing speed and dexterity. The drumming arm was so successful that a version has been designed for drummers who still have both of their real arms. It gives them a third arm attached to their shoulder to improve their playing. Robotic engineers are planning to design new versions of the arm for other musicians and their instruments, too.

Meanwhile, biologists are using robots to learn about animal behavior. They put tiny robots in mazes to see how they navigate through them. The robots' behavior will help scientists better understand the way ants communicate with one another to navigate around obstacles.

By flexing his muscles, drummer Jason Barnes can send signals to his robotic arm to tighten or loosen his grip on his drumsticks.

ARM CAN HOLD TWO STICKS AT ONCE

ROBOTS IN SPACE

Robots continue to be essential in space missions. Remotely operated vehicles (ROVs) are unmanned spacecraft that can travel to distant planets and explore their surfaces. These mobile vehicles can travel freely on wheels or leg-like appendages across a variety of terrains. They can explore, take photographs, and collect samples.

The same kinds of robotic arms that are used in factories can serve astronauts in space by fetching tools, performing tasks too dangerous for humans, and serving as anchors while astronauts work outside their spacecraft. There is even a humanoid robot in development called the Robonaut. It has five-fingered hands and arms that give it humanlike dexterity to perform complicated tasks in space. The Robonaut is fitted with a thermal suit so it can withstand the extreme temperatures of outer space.

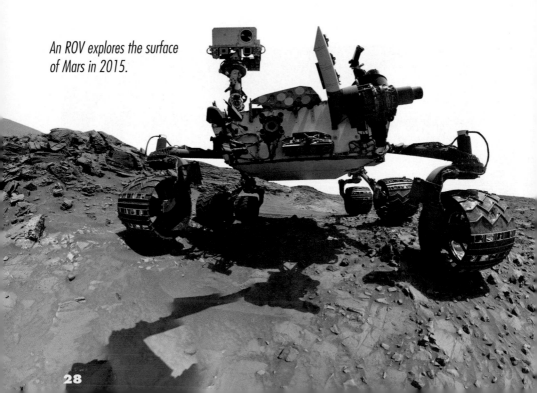

An ROV explores the surface of Mars in 2015.

WHEEL DESIGN ALLOWS ROBOT TO CLIMB STEEP SURFACES

CAMERAS AND SENSORS HELP ROBOT NAVIGATE AND COLLECT INFORMATION

A VolcanoBot explores the interior of the Kilauea volcano in Hawaii.

EXPLORING THE EARTH AND SEA

Just as scientists have sent robots to explore outer space, they are now using them to explore the most extreme areas of our own planet. A wall-climbing robot called VolcanoBot was sent into the crater of the volcano Kilauea in Hawaii. It created a map of the volcano's deepest underground passages. In Alaska, an eight-legged robot called Dante II descended into the Mount Spurr volcano to collect data. The information it collected will help scientists understand the harsh environments on other planets.

Meanwhile, a robotic vehicle called Squishy Fingers has been sent into the ocean to collect pieces of coral. The device's robotic fingers resemble tube worms. They are composed of rubber and fiberglass. They are able to collect samples without damaging fragile coral reefs.

Alpha Dog can carry heavy loads across difficult terrain.

ROBOFISH

University of Washington professor Kristi Morgansen has developed three robot fish with artificial fins that enable them to swim underwater. They can swim together in one direction or separate and go in different directions. "Underwater robots don't need oxygen," says Morgansen. "The only reason they come up to the surface right now is for communication." One day the robofish will be used to track underwater pollution and explore remote areas of the ocean.

The T8X looks and moves much like a real spider.

ROBOT ANIMALS

Scientists have modeled many robots after humans. But in recent years, they have been creating robots that look and act like animals. These **biomimetic** robots, like the animals they are based on, are capable of doing tasks that humanoid robots can't. The Legged Squad Support System (LS3), better known as Alpha Dog, was developed for the U.S. military. It is capable of crossing rough terrain that soldiers and their vehicles can't. Alpha Dog combines the body shapes of a dog, horse, and mule. It can carry up to 400 pounds (181 kilograms) of supplies for troops on the move.

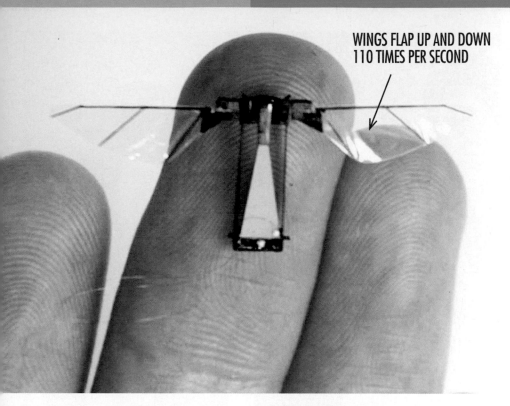

WINGS FLAP UP AND DOWN
110 TIMES PER SECOND

The robotic flies created at Harvard University are small enough to fit comfortably on a fingertip.

ARTIFICIAL BUGS

A robotic fly is being built by researchers at Harvard University's Microrobotics Laboratory. About the size of a common housefly, the robotic fly can squeeze into areas humans cannot reach. It could one day be used to find people trapped under collapsed buildings. Then there's the T8X, a giant robotic spider. Strictly a robotic pet with no practical use, the T8X crawls, creeps, and can even dance! ✺

A researcher conducts tests on a Hiro robot.

WORKING TOGETHER

Until recently, robots were thought to be too disruptive to work in the same factory areas as humans. But that is changing. Japanese inventors have developed a worker robot called Hiro that has sensors to prevent it from bumping into humans or objects.

Hiro is a half humanoid. It has two arms and a humanlike upper body. However, its lower body has wheels to help it move around. It has four "eyes"—two on its face and one on each hand. Because of its sensors, Hiro has been able to work side by side with humans to increase productivity in a number of Japanese industries. Experts predict that by 2018, 60 percent of product assembly factories will have Hiro-type robots working in them.

KEEPING THE PEACE

While the **artificial intelligence** of robots may be limited, their lack of strong human emotions may make them the perfect choice for keeping peace between more hotheaded humans. Research into robotic behavior has led some experts to believe that robot intervention could relieve tension between people and end arguments without violence.

On the other hand, soldier robots could be far more lethal and efficient killers than humans. But soldier robots could also become peacekeepers. Some experts believe that an army of defending robots could discourage aggressive countries from invading. The ongoing development of fighting robots could change the way wars are fought.

A Russian combat robot is equipped with weapons such as guns and grenade launchers.

An engineer makes adjustments to a humanoid robot.

SENSORS POSITIONED LIKE HUMAN EYES

CHAPTER THREE

ON THE JOB

E xperts believe that the market for robotics will reach $1.35 billion by 2019. The largest growth will be in robots used for healthcare and manufacturing. As these new, smarter robots are designed and manufactured to meet growing needs, the industry will require more engineers, **software** developers, researchers, and technicians.

This means there will be many job opportunities for creative people who want to help shape the future of technology. If you are fascinated by robots and what they can be made to do, a career in robotics may be in your future.

RISE OF THE HUMANOIDS

2000

onda releases ASIMO, a two-legged umanoid robot that is capable of nning.

2004

Robosapien, a humanoid robot toy that can be controlled using an infrared remote control or a personal computer, is released.

2014

Manav, a 3D-printed humanoid robot, is produced in India.

SOFTWARE DEVELOPERS

Without software to tell them what to do, robots are just hulks of plastic and metal. Some software tells a robot how to react to different situations, helping it to act on its own. Other programs are used by human operators to directly control a robot's actions. Software developers create these programs. They begin each project by determining which features a piece of software will need. They then design and test programs to meet those goals.

For example, software for an automated vacuum-cleaner robot might tell the robot to take readings from sensors mounted on its body. When the sensors detect an object ahead, the software instructs the robot to turn and avoid it. Developers might make adjustments to the program to change how close the robot gets to an object before turning. Or they might change the speed at which the robot moves.

Dutch developers work on software for a kangaroo-like robot.

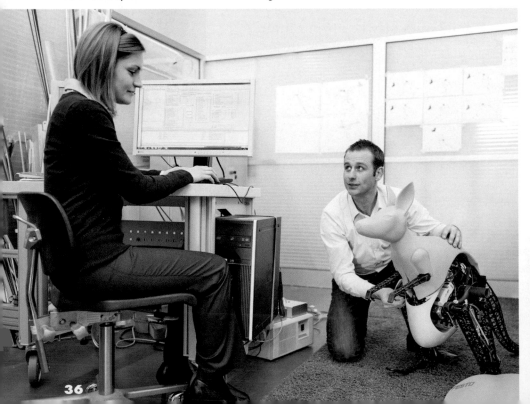

The code created by programmers contains all of the instructions for a robot's behavior.

PROGRAMMERS

Programmers work closely with software developers and are skilled in at least one programming language. Programming languages are ways of writing code that a computer or robot can understand. Programmers take the ideas and designs created by developers and write code containing the actual instructions for the robot.

Programmers are always working to improve their code. They might find **bugs** or ways to make the robot function more smoothly. Even after a robot reaches store shelves, programmers often continue working on its software. They might add new features or solve problems that went unnoticed until more people began using the robot.

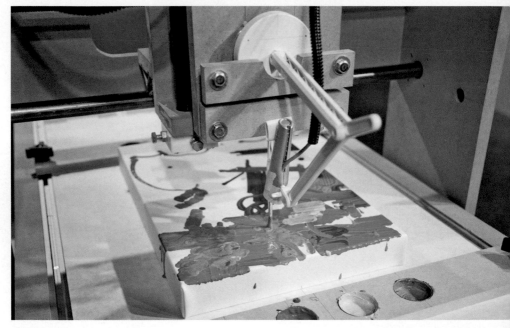

The Interactive Robotic Painting Machine works on one of its creations.

ROBOT ARTISTS

Can robots with artificial intelligence be truly creative? Artist Benjamin Grosser thinks so. His Interactive Robotic Painting Machine creates its own paintings in reaction to sound. The robot's arm holds a paintbrush and moves across a canvas to the sounds it detects. In an art gallery, visitors speak into a microphone. The machine responds to these voices, transforming them into art. When there are no other sounds present, the machine, "like many artists, listens to itself," according to Grosser.

The Interactive Robotic Painting Machine's finished wo often displays interesting patterns and colors.

THE PAINTING FOOL

Computer scientist Simon Colton began working on a computer program called the Painting Fool in 2001. Early versions of the program created artwork by altering photographs that were fed into it. Over time, Colton has improved it to the point that it can create original art without using another image for reference. The Painting Fool has created not only paintings but also three-dimensional sculptures, photographs, and even poetry.

E-DAVID

The Drawing Apparatus for Vivid Interactive Display, or e-David, is the invention of scientists at Germany's University of Konstanz. It was once a welding robot used for manufacturing car parts. Its creators added sensors and a camera to the robot and connected it to a computer. The computer gives e-David drawing commands. It carries out these commands using five brushes and 24 paint colors. Its camera helps the robot learn from its mistakes so it can improve the images it creates. The e-David robot is being used to better understand how human artists work. ✳

The Painting Fool uses its knowledge of art to create images such as this chair.

Japanese engineers test several prototypes of space-exploration robots.

ENGINEERS

Robotics engineers are the creative minds who design robots. They begin by determining what purpose a robot will serve. Does it need to be lightweight? Will it need to travel across a certain kind of terrain? Does it need to withstand a harsh environment? Engineers then design a robot that can meet these challenges.

Once the design is complete, the engineer creates a prototype. The prototype goes through a long testing process. Any problems or kinks must be worked out and corrected before the final robot is built. During this period, the engineers' time is divided between building and testing components in the lab and meeting with other members of the creative team in the office. Engineers are also in charge of designing the machines that are used to manufacture the robot.

TECHNICIANS

Once they are sent out into the world, robots can face many unforeseen problems. They can also break down over time with use, just like any other machine. When this happens, skilled technicians are needed to step in and make repairs. Not just anyone can fix a robot. These machines are very complex and often rely on technology that isn't commonly seen in other devices.

Robotics technicians need to be good at mechanics as well as computer science. Not only can the robot's physical body have problems, but so can its software. Technicians often work closely with engineers and software developers to solve problems. They also test recently repaired robots and perform maintenance to prevent further problems. Most technicians are employed by companies where a malfunctioning robot can seriously affect productivity.

Like all machines, robots require routine maintenance to function properly.

AN INTERVIEW WITH ROBOTICS ENGINEER KEN GOLDBERG

Ken Goldberg is professor of engineering at the University of California, Berkeley, where he directs the AutoLab and is director of the People and Robotics Initiative. He is also an artist who creates artwork using robots.

When did you first realize that you wanted to work with machines and robots? Did any person or event inspire that career choice? In 1969 when the astronauts landed on the moon my parents woke me up to watch it on TV. A few weeks later we got a new refrigerator and I convinced them to put the large cardboard box in the basement. I turned the box into a rocket ship and imagined myself and my friends flying to the moon with it. I really got into making model rockets after that.

What kinds of classes did you take in school to prepare you for your career? I always loved math and science. When I was in high school, a new summer class in computer science for high school juniors began at Lehigh University in my hometown in Pennsylvania. This was 1976 and computers were still new. We worked with punch cards and paper tape. I learned how to program, and when the class ended, I was able to continue programming by logging into the Lehigh computer through our guidance office's computer at school.

What other projects and jobs helped prepare you to work with robots? My experience with computers helped me get summer programming jobs while in college at the University of Pennsylvania. In my junior year, I went to Scotland to study electrical engineering. I vividly remember walking into a room at the University of Edinburgh where they were signing up students for majors. One table advertised "AI (artificial intelligence) and Robotics." I signed up immediately. At the time it was one of the only courses in robotics in the world. It was pure luck that I was there to take advantage of the opportunity.

How important is working in a team in your industry? Does working as part of a team come naturally to you? All my work is collaborative. But that's not a skill that I was taught. The idea of the lone engineer or scientist working alone in a lab is a myth. The ability to work well in teams is essential for science and engineering (and also for many artists).

What projects have you worked on that you're especially proud of? In 1993 when the World Wide Web was just starting, my students and I put the first robot on the Internet. The Telegarden allowed anyone in the world to participate by moving an industrial robot arm to plant and water seeds in a living garden. That idea evolved into something we now call "cloud robotics" where robots use the Internet as a resource for computation and memory. My students and I are working on this with Google and Cisco.

What would your dream project be if you were given unlimited resources? My dream is to provide kids around the world with the means to make and study their own robot. I helped establish the African Robotics Network in Ghana in 2011. We presented a challenge to inventors to make a robot for education that costs $10 or less to make. The grand prize winner was the robot Lollybot, which costs only $8.64 to build. The kids are given the hardware and then assemble their own robot. We want to give Lollybots to kids in Africa and other developing countries such as India and Brazil. The idea is to change the equation to give the world's children the technological know-how they'll need for the 21st century.

What advice would you give to a young person who wants to work in the field of robotics? Draw pictures of robots to imagine what you can make them do. Watch television and movies about robots. There's an excellent new series on PBS called *ANNEdroids*. My six-year-old daughter loves it. The next generation of engineers and designers will create robots that will change the world. ✳

ROBOTICS RESEARCHERS

Robotics researchers are on the cutting edge of new technology in their field. Engineers often rely on researchers to come up with new ideas for robots that they can then design. The ever-expanding field of robotics is constantly looking for robots that can do different tasks. The researchers put in the hard work of finding what those are. They study and test existing robots to see how they can be improved or to provide the blueprint for a new model. They also work to solve problems with robots that aren't as efficient as they could be. When researchers come up with a new concept or idea, they may publish their findings in scientific journals or present them at robotics conferences.

A researcher works with a portable robot.

People who want to work with robots receive training in many scientific fields.

EDUCATION AND TRAINING

Working with robots generally requires a college education. Engineers must have a bachelor's degree in engineering. They may choose to specialize in any number of areas, such as electrical, manufacturing, industrial, or electronics engineering. People who work with software might earn a degree in computer science. Most people in the robotics field also take courses in chemistry, physics, mathematics, and electronics.

During college, students interested in robotics should take advantage of opportunities to do work-study programs and internships. These programs allow students to get on-the-job training before entering the workplace full-time. Learning never stops for the people who design and build robots. They need to keep up with the latest advances in technology by regularly attending conferences, seminars, and training sessions.

With so many new robots hitting the market, it takes a special creation to stand out and become a success.

CHAPTER FOUR

A ROBOT IN THE MAKING

B uilding a new type of robot is a long and complicated process. First, the design must be planned, and then prototypes are built and tested. Adjustments are made to prototypes, and the final robot is at last manufactured at a cost that makes it both affordable to consumers and profitable for the manufacturer. Along the way, the robot's creators face a nearly limitless range of potential issues. Imagine for a moment that you are an inventor working at a robotics company. You come up with an exciting idea for a new kind of robot. What will it take to make your robotics dreams a reality?

GAME-PLAYING ROBOTS

1992	1997	1999	2007
The initial FIRST Robotics Competition is held in the United States.	Deep Blue, an IBM computer that can play chess, defeats world chess champion Garry Kasparov.	Sony releases AIBO, a robotic dog that can be taught to do tricks.	Topio, a humanoid robot that can play Ping-Pong, is built in Vietnam.

Holding brainstorming meetings is a great way to come up with new ideas.

A BOARD GAME ROBOT

You start by meeting with your creative team of engineers and designers. It is time for a brainstorming session about a new robot for the home market. You think about how you love to play board games with your friends. But what do you do when no one is around to play with you? Is there some way you could enjoy your favorite board games by yourself? What if there was a robot you could play against?

The team loves your idea of a game-playing robot. Your company's market researcher looks to see if there are any robots like this that are already in stores. She finds that such a robot does not yet exist. Your designers work up some drawings of what this robot might look like. The engineers work out what components it will need to function.

STEP BY STEP

One robot design attracts your attention more than the others. It has a humanoid body. This makes sense, as the robot will be a companion for its user. The robot has an extended torso and large head, but no legs. It won't need them because it will be sitting when it plays. It has wheels for "feet" so it can be moved around easily. Its arms and hands are able to pick up cards, move markers across a board, and complete other actions required when playing board games. A computer-driven speaking mechanism will give the robot a voice so it can speak with its owner. The last big question to answer is whether this robot can be made inexpensively enough so people will want to buy it. You review the figures with your financial department, and they give the project a green light. It's time to build a prototype!

The most advanced humanoid robots have hands and fingers that move just like a real person's.

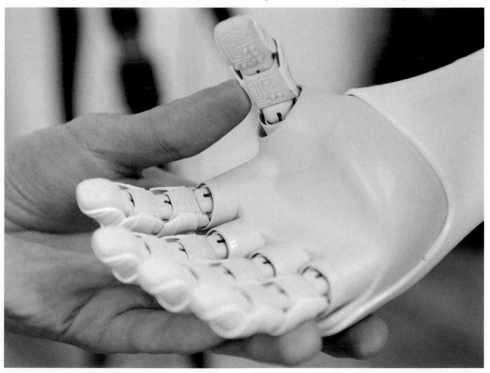

A FIRST Robotics Competition team makes adjustments to its robot before a competition.

ROBOT GAMES

For many young people, robot competitions serve as an important introduction to making and operating robots. In these competitions, people build their own robots and use them to play a variety of games or to solve problems.

VEX COMPETITIONS

VEX Competitions are some of the most exciting robotics events. Teams of two to four students work together to build robots and then compete against other teams. A different competition takes place each year. For the

2015–2016 competition, called Nothing but Net, students built vehicular robots to launch balls into nets and score goals, like robotic basketball.

FIRST ROBOTICS COMPETITION

The FIRST (For Inspiration and Recognition of Science and Technology) Robotics Competition is an international contest for high school students. The initial FIRST competition was held in 1992. Today, there are more than 3,000 FIRST teams from 19 countries. High schoolers and their teachers receive parts from FIRST to help them build their robots. They are also encouraged to

Huge crowds gather to watch FIRST Robotics events.

Robot Wars competitors tried to design robots that could not easily be flipped over or broken.

create their own specialized accessories. Some FIRST competitions have included robots that flew discs into goals. Others have required competitors to create robots capable of shooting basketballs into hoops.

BATTLING BOTS

Some robot competitions have pitted robots against each other in battle. Robot Wars, an event held in the 1990s for adult hobbyists, inspired a television game show in England. A U.S. show, *BattleBots*, had a similar premise. Competitors designed and operated armed robot machines that would battle each other in an arena. The show returned to the air in 2015, proving you can't keep a good fighting robot down. ✳

DOWN TO WORK

As you move forward with a prototype, you hire a software development company to create programs for your robot. At first the software will only be able to play several of the most popular board games, such as chess and checkers. You plan to add support for more games after the robot is released. The software is designed so users will be able to download updates for new board games to their computers. They can then transfer the updates to the robot using a cable.

Your designers decide on the best materials to use in building the prototype. They determine that it is best to use plastic for the hands, arms, and face to give the robot a humanlike appearance and flexibility. To make the robot's body strong, they will support it with metal pieces. Your game-playing robot is coming together very nicely. Now it's time to test it and see how it works.

An engineer assembles a robot by hand at a factory in Canada.

Designing something as complex as a robotic hand might require a long process of experimenting and making changes to prototypes.

TESTING AND TWEAKING

The first tests of your prototype reveal some problems with the design. You find that the robot's computerized voice is too high-pitched, making it annoying to hear. It will have to be reprogrammed to be more pleasant sounding. Also, the robot is so good at some games that it is hard for beginners to win. You decide to add several difficulty levels for each game to make sure all users can have fun with the robot.

You also find out quickly that the plastic used to make the robot's hands breaks easily. To solve this, your engineers find a material that is more durable. However, it will cost more to produce. You will need to find a way to reduce the cost of some other part of the robot to make up for this change.

Workers build Ford automobiles on an assembly line in 1930.

THE ASSEMBLY LINE

While robots are the main workforce in many factories today, the assembly line they labor on was invented more than a century earlier. Before the Industrial Revolution of the 19th century, products were made by hand, with skilled craftspeople creating individual parts. When all the parts were finished, the product was put together. Inventor Eli Whitney popularized the concept of producing standard, interchangeable parts that unskilled workers could assemble. As a result, Whitney's gun factory turned out weapons quickly and cheaply.

OLDS AND FORD LEAD THE WAY

The first true assembly line was created by carmaker Ransom Olds in 1901. Olds's "horseless carriage" was moved from one work station to another. At each station, workers added a certain set of parts to the vehicle. The assembly line boosted the company's productivity by 500 percent in just one year. Rival carmaker Henry Ford improved on Olds's idea by putting cars on a conveyer belt to move them more quickly from station to station. The time it took to produce one Ford Model T car shrunk from one and a half days to just 90 minutes.

Ransom Olds operates one of his cars in 1901.

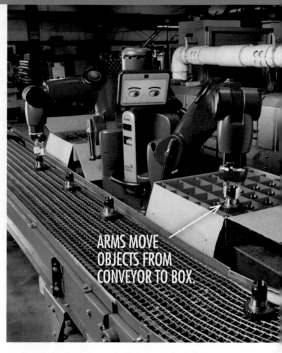

ARMS MOVE OBJECTS FROM CONVEYOR TO BOX.

Stations on modern assembly lines are often operated by robots.

ENTER THE ROBOT

The next big innovation in assembly lines came with the invention of robots. General Motors brought a robotic arm to its assembly line in 1961. In recent years, robots have replaced humans altogether in many factories. Newer robots, such as Rethink Robotics' Baxter, launched in 2012, can perform many tasks on the assembly line with as much skill as any human worker. Today, even robots are built by other robots! ☀

A good name and logo help new robots stand out on store shelves.

MARKETING

Before final production of your robot can begin, you need a good marketing plan. This will inform potential customers what your robot is and hopefully make them interested in buying it. Part of the marketing plan is coming up with a catchy name for your robot. One member of your marketing team suggests the name Gamebot, but you don't think it's catchy enough. Instead, you name it BoardBot, because it plays board games. You will advertise BoardBot on hobby Web sites and social media so people who like to play board games will see it. You set a price for your robot that is reasonable enough to sell it but high enough to make a profit. Meanwhile, your prototype has passed the latest tests with flying colors. It is time to begin production.

AYORKOR KORSAH

Ayorkor Korsah grew up in Ghana but went to school in the United States, where she earned a doctorate in robotics and artificial intelligence from Carnegie Mellon University. She is now a teacher of robotics at Ashesi University College in Ghana. She also runs the Ashesi Innovation Experience, a summer program that teaches robotics and leadership to high school students.

READY TO ROLL

Skilled technicians and other workers assemble BoardBots piece by piece at your company's robotics factory. Some of the heavier and more difficult labor on the assembly line is done by other robots. At the same time, technical writers begin creating the precise and easy-to-understand instructions that owners will need.

Once assembled, the robots are boxed and shipped to various stores across the country. A few weeks pass, and the sales figures that come in are excellent. In an increasingly crowded robotics marketplace, BoardBot is a winner. But this is no time for a vacation. You immediately start thinking about your next project. How about a robot that can play catch? Back to the drawing board!

Robots even play an important role in manufacturing other robots.

SMALLER ROBOT
PRODUCED AT FACTORY

LARGE ROBOT CARRIES
HEAVY LOADS WITHOUT
A HUMAN DRIVER

A self-driving car is tested on city streets in Japan in 2015.

ROAD ROBOTS

In the future, robots could be involved in nearly every aspect of our lives. They will even drive our cars. Self-driving cars are already being tested and could change the way we live. Commuters will no longer have to pay attention to traffic on the way to work. Parking lots will be replaced by open green space, as the cars will be able to move along and pick up new passengers instead of waiting for their drivers. Without humans behind the wheel, auto accidents will become a rarity. Ships piloted by robots may also soon be sailing the seas.

SMALLER AND SMALLER

While industrial robots get bigger and bigger, other robots will shrink in size. Tiny rescue robots will enter disaster areas too dangerous or difficult for humans and large robots. They will use sensors and cameras to locate victims and report on them to rescue teams. Even smaller "nanobots" will be injected into the human body's bloodstream to cure diseases.

NEW CHALLENGES

As more specialized robots are designed in the years to come, will humans find themselves out of jobs? In a recent survey, experts were divided in their opinions. On the positive side, they felt that as robots become more prevalent, new businesses will emerge to keep people working. Other people whose workload is lessened due to robotic help will find themselves with more time for leisure pursuits, family activities, and self-improvement. "Historically, technology has created more jobs than it destroys," says Vinton Cerf, a vice president at Google, "and there is no reason to think otherwise in this case." A robotic revolution is coming, and it could mean a better life for all of us. ✳

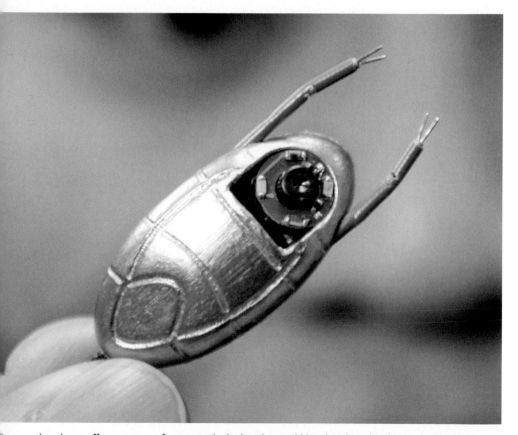

A researcher shows off a prototype of a tiny medical robot that could be placed inside a human body to treat diseases such as cancer.

CAREER STATS

ELECTRICAL AND ELECTRONICS ENGINEERS

MEDIAN ANNUAL SALARY (2015): $95,230

NUMBER OF JOBS (2014): 315,900

PROJECTED JOB GROWTH (2014–2024): 0%, little or no change

PROJECTED INCREASE IN JOBS (2014–2024): –100

REQUIRED EDUCATION: Bachelor's degree

LICENSE/CERTIFICATION: May be required for some positions

ELECTROMECHANICAL TECHNICIANS

MEDIAN ANNUAL SALARY (2015): $53,340

NUMBER OF JOBS (2014): 14,700

PROJECTED JOB GROWTH (2014–2024): 1%, little or no change

PROJECTED INCREASE IN JOBS (2014–2024): 100

REQUIRED EDUCATION: Associate's degree

LICENSE/CERTIFICATION: Possibly postsecondary certificate

SOFTWARE DEVELOPERS

MEDIAN ANNUAL SALARY (2015): $100,690

NUMBER OF JOBS (2014): 1,114,000

PROJECTED JOB GROWTH (2014–2024): 17%, much faster than average

PROJECTED INCREASE IN JOBS (2014–2024): 186,600

REQUIRED EDUCATION: Bachelor's degree

LICENSE/CERTIFICATION: None

Figures reported by the United States Bureau of Labor Statistics

RESOURCES

BOOKS

Ceceri, Kathy. *Making Simple Robots: Exploring Cutting-Edge Robotics with Everyday Stuff.* San Francisco: Maker Media, 2015.

Furstinger, Nancy. *Helper Robots.* Minneapolis: Lerner Publications, 2015.

Mara, Wil. *Robotics: From Concept to Consumer.* New York: Scholastic, 2015.

Swanson, Jennifer. *National Geographic Kids: Everything Robotics.* Washington, DC: National Geographic, 2016.

FACTS FOR NOW

Visit this Scholastic Web site for more information on making robots:
www.factsfornow.scholastic.com
Enter the keywords **Making Robots**

GLOSSARY

animal therapy (AN-uh-muhl THER-uh-pee) the use of animals to calm and improve the lives of the disabled and the elderly by their presence

artificial intelligence (ahr-tuh-FISH-uhl in-TEL-i-juhns) the science of making computers do things that previously needed human intelligence, such as understanding language

automatons (aw-TAH-muh-tahnz) mechanical devices designed to perform a physical function, often one that is repetitive

autonomous (aw-TAH-nuh-muhs) able to act independently

biomimetic (bye-oh-mih-MEH-tik) imitating or copying the behavior of living things

bugs (BUHGZ) errors in a computer program

humanoid (HYOO-muh-noyd) having human form or a robot or other device with a human shape or traits

prostheses (prahs-THEE-sees) artificial devices that replace a missing body part

prototype (PROH-toh-type) an early version of an invention that tests an idea to see if it will work

sensors (SEN-surz) instruments that can detect a physical quality such as light or motion and transmit the information to a controlling device

software (SAWFT-wair) computer programs that control the workings of the equipment, or hardware, and direct it to do specific tasks

thermostat (THER-muh-stat) a device that establishes and maintains a desired temperature automatically

INDEX

Page numbers in *italics* indicate illustrations.

INDEX *(CONTINUED)*

ABOUT THE AUTHOR

STEVEN OTFINOSKI has written more than 180 books for young readers, including books on the history of television, computers, and rockets. This is his seventh book in the Calling All Innovators series. He lives in Connecticut with his family.